A Note from the Author

I'VE BEEN A CAREGIVER MY ENTIRE ADULT LIFE. First I helped care for my grandparents. Then I helped with Mom when, at age 63, she had a stroke. When Dad showed increasing signs of Alzheimer's disease, I was able to adjust my career and other responsibilities to move across the country to help care for my parents. Mom passed on in 2013, and then I served as executor of my oldest sister's estate when she passed on a year later. Dad is 93 and lives with me.

Every day I make a conscious choice to care. The well-meaning question I often hear from people is: "How do you do it?" I wonder: *How could I* not *do it?* As challenging as caregiving can be, I believe strongly in what I do because I am giving back to those who cared for our family and because I know it is the right thing to do. No regrets.

I find caregiving extremely fulfilling. With each experience, I learn and grow as a person. Happiness, love, warmth, closeness, and contentment are vital components of my caregiving experience.

But that doesn't deny the reality: Caregiving can be stressful and tiring.

As caregivers, we give of ourselves every day. It's important for us to find time to take a break to restore and renew. I liken it to my car—I have to keep filling the tank; I don't expect it to run on empty! I can't expect myself to do so either.

Coloring is a *great* way to fill our tanks. Coloring can be done anytime, practically anywhere. We can do it in short bursts when we need a mini break, or for longer spans of time when we are in need of some deeper relaxation. Coloring has been shown to reduce stress and lower anxiety, and it allows us to be more mindful and relaxed in the moment. For me, coloring is a little escape, allowing me to relieve stress and remember who I am.

Because, as each of us knows, caregiving is just one part of who we are. When we give ourselves the gift of creative moments, it's a reminder of the many colors that make up the unique portrait of who we are.

Every day is a blank canvas, and it's up to us to paint the day with colors of our choosing. It is my hope that this book inspires you to paint your days with the colors of kindness, joy, and positivity, and that it offers you a restorative way for you to fill your own tank each and every day.

Thank you for all you do to care for others. May you be well on your caregiving journey!

Amy Goyer, Author,
Juggling Life, Work and Caregiving
Connect on *Twitter.com/amygoyer, Facebook.com/AmyGoyer1, amygoyer.com*

Coloring Tools and Tips

COLORED PENCILS: With a variety of shapes and sizes, colored pencils are great for shading or blending colors together, both of which add interest and depth to any design.

GEL PENS AND MARKERS: Magic markers and gel pens are good for adding bold, defined bursts of color.

CRAYONS: A staple of any household with kids, crayons are surprisingly versatile when filling in large spaces.

TIP: Add a piece of scrap paper under each page you're working on to make sure that the color doesn't bleed through the page.

Choose Your Colors

You can use both complementary and analogous colors to make a gorgeous piece of art—the possibilities are as endless as your imagination.

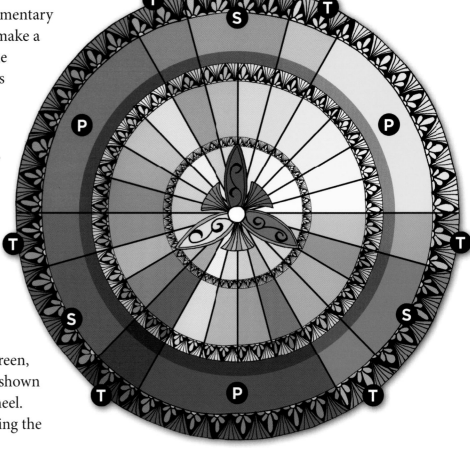

PRIMARY COLORS

The primary colors—red, yellow, and blue—are denoted by a "P" on the outside of the color wheel. Primary colors cannot be created by mixing any other colors.

SECONDARY COLORS

The secondary colors—green, orange, and purple—are shown by an "S" on the color wheel. These are formed by mixing the primary colors.

TERTIARY COLORS

Yellow-orange, red-orange, red-purple, blue-purple, blue-green, and yellow-green make up the tertiary colors, which are noted with a "T" on the outside of the wheel. These colors are formed by mixing a primary color with a secondary color.

Inspiration Is All Around You

NOT SURE WHAT COLORS TO USE? You can find a rainbow of inspiration all around you in your daily life. Take a few minutes each day to look and to really notice the patterns of different plants and animals, the colors of the flowers that dot your street, and the radiant hues of the sunset or the morning sky. By being more mindful of the colors that make up your day, you can make them come alive in your own creations. Get inspired by the designs on the following page, too. As you can see, each artist lends his or her own style and personality to the artwork. One person may choose sunny yellows, another may pick soft teals, and another will add background doodles. There is no right way or wrong way to approach any page—the key is to enjoy the moment and your unique creations that result!

A Note from the Illustrator

THANK YOU for allowing my artwork to be the canvas for your coloring adventures. Most adventures need some directions, so here are mine:

1. Pick a page.
2. Pick a medium.
3. Play.

I created every illustration with that third instruction in mind because what's the point of a coloring book if you can't have fun with it? Each page is filled with details, which you can approach in many ways. You can color each tiny shape or you can group them together into bigger sections. You can leave parts blank for pops of white space and play with different tones and hues.

Each page is designed to stir your imagination and help you unwind into your own creative space. The right way to use this book is your way, and I encourage you to have fun and enjoy the creative process.

j. clementwall

Judy Clement Wall is a writer and artist who has illustrated several coloring books, including *Inkspirations for Mindful Living, Inkspirations for Women, Inkspirations Create While You Wait,* and the creative self-love journal *Find Your Awesome.* She also creates unique cards and artwork that celebrate life. Visit her at: *www.judyclementwall.com.*

Colored by Makena Vargo.

Colored by Robyn Henoch.

Colored by Marsy Festa.

Colored by Robyn Henoch.

Colored by Kim Weiss.

Colored by Amanda Collins.

Colored by Allison Janse.

Colored by Lawna Patterson Oldfield.

Colored by Makena Vargo.

Colored by Argelyn McLean.

Colored by Makena Vargo.

Caring for others fills my heart

and makes me stronger.

—Amy Goyer

Caregiving often calls us
to lean into love we didn't
know possible.

—*Tia Walker*

lean into love

Every sunrise is an invitation to

brighten someone's day.

—Richelle E. Goodrich

Flowers leave some of their fragrance

in the hand that bestows them.

—*Chinese Proverb*

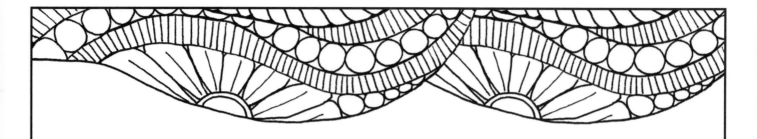

Success is a journey,

not a destination.

—Arthur Ashe

It is not how much we do,

but how much love we put in the doing.

It is not how much we give,

but how much love is

put in the giving.

—*Mother Teresa*

The present moment is
filled with joy and happiness.
If you are attentive, you will see it.

—Thich Nhat Hahn

The things I do matter.

They have had a positive effect on my

loved ones and, I believe, in a bigger sense,

I have contributed to the stream

of love in this world.

—Amy Goyer

Compassion brings us to a stop,

and for a moment we rise

above ourselves.

—Mason Cooley

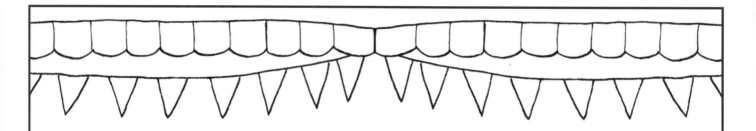

Do the best that you can in the place

where you are, and be kind.

—Scott Nearing

As much as you try,

you will never be perfect.

You are a human being who is

doing the best you can—

and that is enough!

—*Amy Goyer*

And it is still true,

no matter how old you are,

when you go out into the world

it is best to hold hands

and stick together.

—Robert Fulghum

There are two ways of spreading light:

to be the candle or

the mirror that reflects it.

—*Edith Warton*

One may walk over the highest mountain

one step at a time.

—John Wanamaker

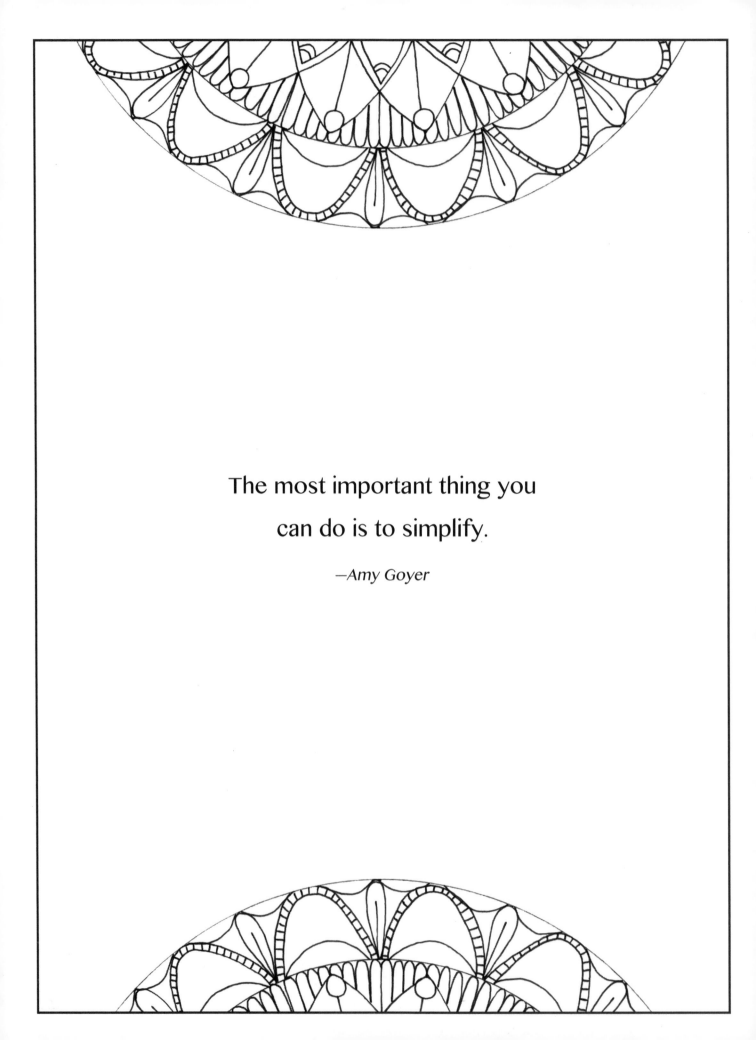

The most important thing you
can do is to simplify.

—Amy Goyer

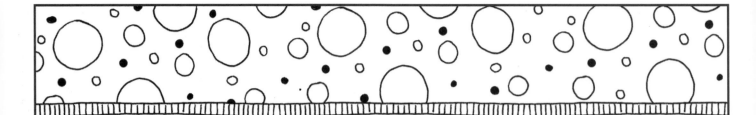

Life is a balance of holding on

and letting go.

—*Rumi*

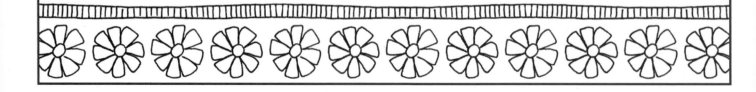

Some days there won't be

a song in your heart.

Sing anyway.

—*Emory Austin*

Those who bring sunshine to
the lives of others cannot keep it
from themselves.

—*J.M. Barrie*

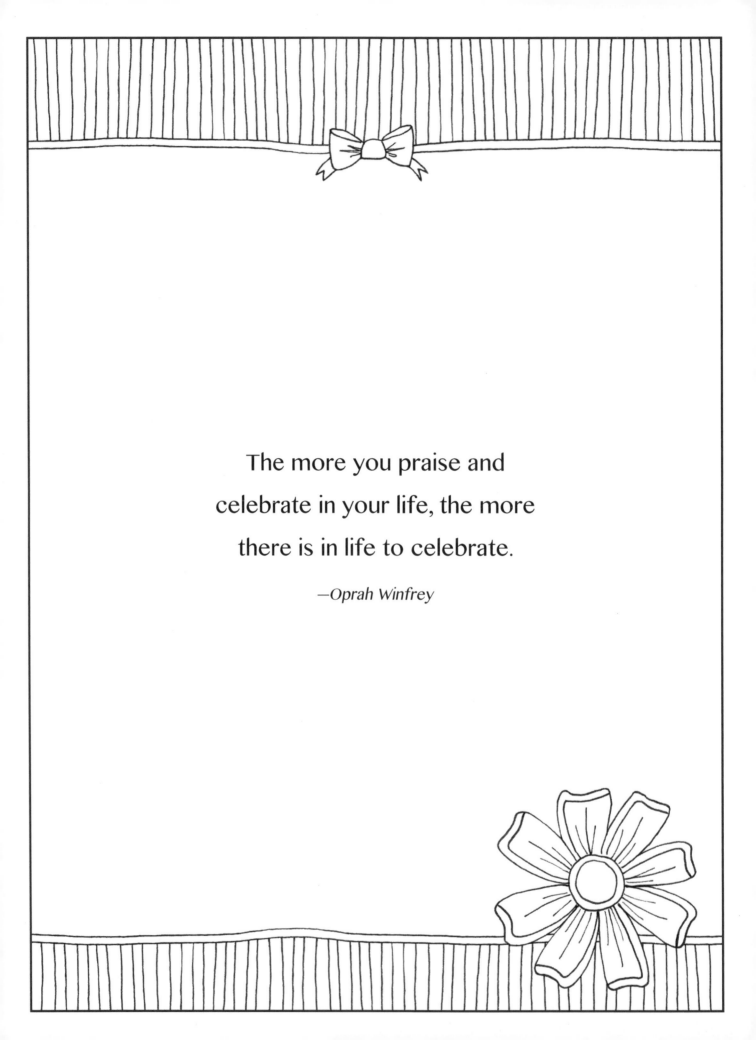

The more you praise and
celebrate in your life, the more
there is in life to celebrate.

—*Oprah Winfrey*

Being of service,

as imperfect as my care is,

has meaning, and that

feels good.

—Amy Goyer

The little things?

The little moments?

They aren't little.

—Jon Kabat-Zinn

If you want to lift yourself up,

lift up someone else.

—Booker T. Washington

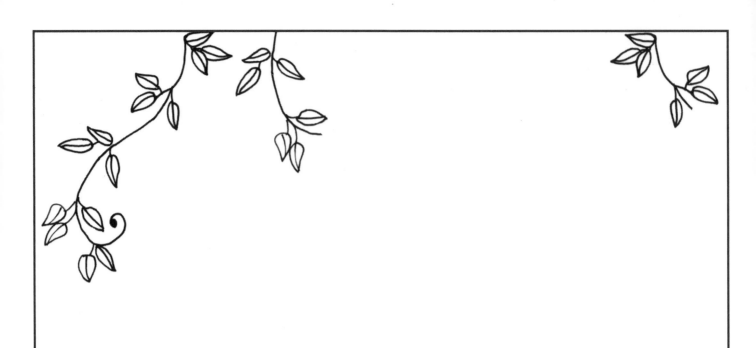

Wherever you are,

be there totally.

—*Eckhart Tolle*

Perhaps the most important lesson
I've learned is that my goal is not to prevent change;
it will invariably happen. My goal, instead,
is to ride the waves of change.

—Amy Goyer

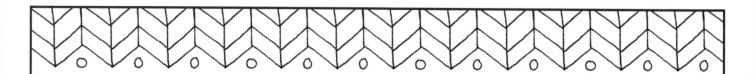

I am convinced that life is

10 percent what happens to me and

90 percent how I react to it.

—*Charles Swindoll*

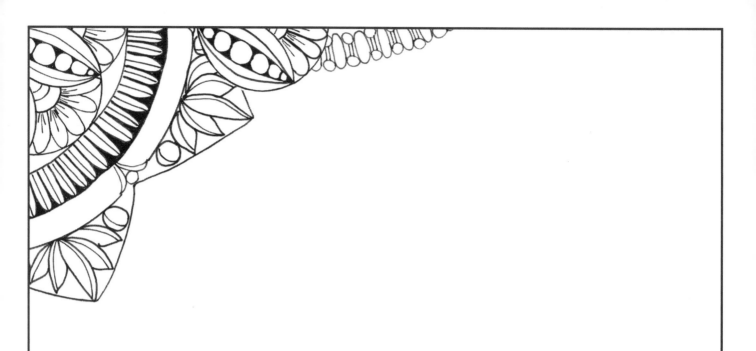

We are what we think.

All that we are arises with our thoughts.

With our thoughts we make the world.

—*Gautama Buddha*

Being deeply loved by someone
gives you strength,
while loving someone deeply
gives you courage.

—*Lao Tzu*

They may forget your name,

but will never forget how you made them feel.

—*Maya Angelou*

A flower is a weed seen

through joyful eyes.

—Jonathan Lockwood Huie

Gratitude and attitude are not challenges;

they are choices.

—*Robert Braathe*

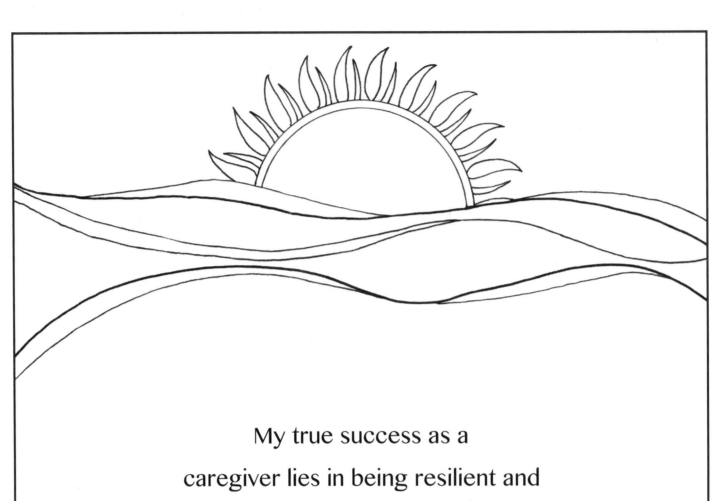

My true success as a

caregiver lies in being resilient and

being fully, lovingly present on

this unpredictable journey.

—*Amy Goyer*